Primitive Mentor

PITT POETRY SERIES
ED OCHESTER, EDITOR

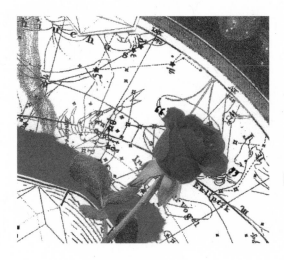

Primitive Mentor

Dean Young

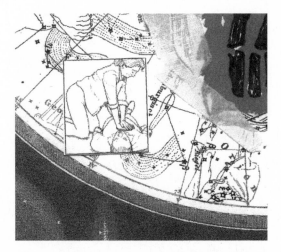

UNIVERSITY
OF
PITTSBURGH
PRESS

Published by the University of Pittsburgh Press, Pittsburgh, PA 15260

Copyright © 2008, Dean Young

All rights reserved

Manufactured in the United States of America

Printed on acid-free paper

10 9 8 7 6 5 4 3 2 1

ISBN 13: 978-0-8229-5991-5

ISBN 10: 0-8229-5991-7

for Matt Hart & Dobby Gibson

CONTENTS

4

****

Primitive Mentor

Dear Reader

This constant plumbing of the spirit—
like living in a mine making a study

of cave-ins. What thrives down there
doesn't need eyes, just electrified skin,

super-touchy body that's one big ear.
A pebble's prevarication is a mariachi band,

whisper your own name, it's a warning screamed.
I don't think I'll be back soon,

not that I was ever here. Too often
we are left to piece together the sensibility

wounded by such perceptions, someone burying
an animal not oft interred,

someone persisting with an absurd hat,
the steady reduction of the story

to the sentence, syntax to end-stop,
punctuation to New Year's Eve bash

in a black hole. Care for an organ donation?
A moonshine absolution thins

to demoted Pluto glow, one shadow
kicking another's ass. Be we just passing

figments in this waterhead world or
is there hope that you and I may leave

some trace more permanent, scarlet,
tooth-marked, at least upon each other's heart?

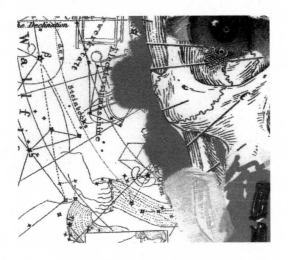

What Form after Death

What form after death will we take,
a gizmo birdie like William Butler Yeats?
I doubt it. How about a doorstop bunny
like the one we saw in Charleston, wanted
but didn't have the money? Heavy enough
to be made of lead, paint rubbed off its head
by petting, no gust strong enough to slam
what it kept open. Nope, the rain comes
in mirages shredded, I don't know where
any of us are headed, a furnace
of ectoplasmic metallurgy or compost pit
of worms working between hermaphroditic
orgies? Dear mustachioed Aunt Gloria who
gave me 20 bucks to blow on rubber snakes
and pinball, what became of you? Small stone
rubbed smaller by the wave's surge? Birthday song
becomes a dirge, the soldier's poem quaint words
on crumbling paper. Is that what you were
telling me when you didn't know who?
I'd be the last to insist my mother
didn't have conversations with my father
on the TV set after he was dead. Sometimes
I too hope to return, make some mischief
at our favorite restaurant, snuff some candles
and whisper how much I love you
if you're still around. And Stan Rice, now just
7 or 8 books no one talks about but
when I reread still frighten me
into delight. Maybe all that we become
is rhyme of our limited time alive,
an echo loosening almost no snow,
no avalanche, just some puffs of white
like clouds that seem like nothing
until the pilot hits one.

Disappearing Ink

is only as good as the secret of its reappearance.
It may take some time to sink in
unless it never does, just pools on the surface,
I love you you'll never know.
But none of that matters now,
like kissing someone asleep,
we're all in too big a hurry, you
with your blitzkrieg party-planner,
me with my puppy who has to go.
Surely an explanation of all this botheration
is forthcoming, why the web-footed girl
hates water and the president is a moron.
Will smoke make it appear? Noxious gas?
Another detonation? It seems the whole plot
hinges on a letter either never written or received,
some singer insisting on hopelessness cross-
purposes to her five-octave range. May one day
soon someone pull us out into the rain
where all that vanished becomes legible again
and all we've struggled to decipher fades away at last.

Washing in Cold Water

I don't think I'm close enough
to start giving everything away yet.
Maybe I'll spend one more day in the madhouse
reading them Hopkins and Breton for corroboration.
Until you come back inside with a bunch of loonies,
each of them carrying a leaf,
I don't think you're ready
and I'm not ready.
Achilles was ready.
Wordsworth was ready but when he asked directions,
a man pointed behind him at the mist
and said he'd already crossed the peak.
It's probably not the peak or the valley
where you put down your day-pack
and order the thick local beer.
It's probably not some sort of sexual mania
brought on by ogling the floor show.
Or dissections.
Glaciers dragged most of the landscape here
then the wind wore faces in it.
On the plains, who kills who
is impossible to keep straight
then Achilles' son marries Helen's daughter
and a flock of lambs covers the hills
and a sapling's roots slowly crush
a skeleton of a cat buried under it.
The parents can't decide when to tell their child
she was found in a dumpster so never do.
Of course that's not the end of it.
Her whole life, teachers praise her,
but something in the mirror drifts.
The wondrous is the truth because it's simpler.
My mother tried to be nice to me
but she had to lock me in my room.
That's not an excuse.
I heard doves.

Self Search

When we look around for proof
of basic epistemological matters,
that life isn't only seemings smattered,
a dream brought on by snaggled meat,
often the self blocks the view
of the tree or cat or car race
so all we find are me-leaves, me-meows,
me-machines of speedy impulse-me.
Maybe the point's to see the self
as a kind of film that tints everything
bluer, more you-er and yet look through,
whatever you have to do, volunteer
at a shelter changing the abandoned
hamster's litter, put together a coat drive
for the poor, go door to door for your candidate,
be devoted to a lover or lose yourself
cheering in a crowd, Go Hens! Go
higher, go lower, to see perhaps the sky
as a rock might, meditate until you become
a beam of light, be divided as a 3 by 27
and not get overcome by your identity ending
or expect to reappear after the decimal.
Perhaps you should be practicing not having
a self to claim, one day it's baggage
we're without, no longer waiting
for it to squirt out onto the conveyor belt
with all the others that look so much alike.
Yet it is sad to imagine no me around
to press his nose into your sleeping hair.
I worry death won't care, just a bunch of dust
rushing up, some addled flashes, chills
then nil. I like too much that old idea
of heaven, everyone and pet you've lost
runs up which could not happen
if there's no me there to greet.

Self, I'm stuck with you
but the notion of becoming unglued is too much
and brings tears that come, of course,
because you're such a schmuck. Some days
you crash about raving how ignored you are
then why the hell don't people let you alone
but I've seen you too perform small
nobilities, selfless generosities.
One way or the other, we'll part I'm sure
and you'll take me with you?

The Great Loneliness

Everyone had heard of the Great Loneliness
but no one could be sure they had it,
it's impossible to talk about
and comparisons are useless,
like trying to judge butterflies by weight.
You could be folding towels still warm from the dryer
and suffering the Great Loneliness
or suffering falling short of the Great Loneliness
which is like the suffering of crofters
in 18th-century novels,
there only to reveal some aspect of character
in the real players. You might as well
be lunching at the health club
as holding yourself together in a maelstrom.
You could be a boy who drove a rusty nail
into your foot and now must stay inside
listening to his friends play tag
or a woman fingering her pearls while
chattering about the adulteries of celebrities.
Maybe you only kissed the impossible one twice
for the rosebush to send its thorns
through your insides but still, no knowing.
And your friend, the expert, who turned her freezer
into a diorama of failed arctic expeditions
and likes to stand under a waterfall
and scream, even she can't be sure.
There are tests of course, autopsies,
an unusual hollowness in long bones,
a bubble in the oblongata
but by then what does it matter
when you'll never be lonely again,
that puppy who ran into the rain,
it wasn't your fault, licking your face?

Gruss

Whenever I'm not drunk enough
is a waste of time.
I carry within me a hypnagogic dawn,
maybe the insulation gnawed by rats,
maybe I'll never be back.
Ha ha to the mating swans.
Ha ha to the sepulchral golden slime
that shines and shines and shines.
This party started long before I arrived
with the last of wacko youthful chatter,
a curious crew, prone to slam-dance depression.
What's the matter? Don't know, maybe so
much hilarity is a strain on us or at least
we like to boast in loopy communiqués
to those who've seen through us
and love us for what they see,
maybe some trees, a packing factory,
some secretive birdie hopping about
with a grasshopper in its mouth.
I don't know what I'd do without you
although that's how I spend most of my time.
It'd be unbearable otherwise,
like a vacation without sleeping pills,
without some creaking rain
abating the granite's breakdown.
Such a paltry gesture, my surrender.

Look at Quintillions Ripen'd & Look at Quintillions Green

How impossible to have a reasonable relation
with the self no matter what you say, Walt Whitman.
You don't seem all that reasonable either,
half libidinous ether, half dirt soldiers bleed into,
half lilac branch. Three halves?
Precisely my point. Self, one moment
you're a mountain with no roads or road signs,
your thoughts higher than air
so all the climbers can do is stare
and shield their eyes from your glacier glare
then kerplunk, you're demoted,
flunked, a sticky splot on a tabletop
so the waitress comes over
with her table-wiping rag
of such rude condition it's hard to imagine
anything it wipes is ever better off.
Sorry, she doesn't apologize but doesn't not either,
an irony perfected by working beneath yourself
like tightrope walkers mending nets.
But she too is part of particle physics,
too complicated for most of us to fathom,
here one moment, there the next
without it seems any intermediate fix
like the self's mood swings, all over- or under-
whelmed, never just plain whelmed.
Not that I'm asking for some steady boring state
of never going up and never sliding down.
If we admit that constant orgasm
ain't gonna happen in our current contraption,
there's bound to be some down time,
refractory torpors reading a back issue
of *Sporting Life* in the waiting room
while the drops dilate your eyes
and the words about fly-tying blur
then are consumed with light too bright to see by.

The mind is a tiny island you've washed up on.
You wanted to win the million dollars.
You wanted to be the teacher of futuristic poetries
not the structure of the argument.
In your future is a long journey.
A mansion with many bathrooms.
Something dark on the moors.
Spangle.

Mannerist

It is said a hole knocked in the ceiling
of the flat Caravaggio fled, skipping rent,
explains the light source of those late works.
The problem for the authorities, a lot
of pissed-off swordsmen, was catching him
and we can only guess someone finally did
as his body was never found. Constant
in this world are the problems of landlords
and lighting and the sense of something out
to get you. I tried to solve the death-rattle-
in-the-middle-of-the-night problem by draining
the radiators, the encroaching-shadows-
every-moment-your-last predicament by reaching
way out the window and sawing off the spooky
scratching branch. Because of what I read
about consciousness and death, I did not
intervene but watched the broken bird grind
its eye in the sidewalk then I turned
away, un-mercy killing. I tried to solve
the why-am-I-so-dumb problem by reading books
I couldn't understand. How about just leaving
it all alone, not getting out of bed,
the problem itself perplexed by a plethora
of variables: tax bracket, traffic pattern,
therapeutic workshop. Exhausting failure,
waste of raw materials, disastrous dis-
proportion like forever adolescence. Just
lying in the innocent-seeming gloxinias,
you can't go forward and you can't go back
and staying still ain't an option. Perhaps
it's best to embrace a what-the-heck philosophy.
Put some words in the word balloon, hardly
matters what as the cartoon concerns a conversation

between a trashcan and a duck. It's spring
in another week. You're not so awfully off
after all. The heart is drawn from its yellow tub
still beating.

My Outlook on Life

It's good to have a strongman as governor,
makes everyone else seem weak, even industrialists.
And skull ornaments are nice, so too roadside
attractions of two-headed animals if they're not
pickled in formaldehyde. Some people get wetter
than others in the rain which corresponds
to my outlook on life, one of 'em. Another
is you can't trust ducks or public transit.
Another is people must always be allowed avenues
of escape that can be perked up with colorful
names. Rue of Laughing Livers. Boulevard Rimbaud
where Rimbaud was beaten and arrested. Shoppes
of supercilious, useless objects that trigger
repressed erotic needs, wicker birdcages,
dragon kites, Chinese handcuffs, bullwhips,
qat to chew, a maker of masks who starts
with a cast of your face so on the inside
it feels like you're wearing your actual face
only you don't mind scaring children, relish
their thinking you're some mythical beast, maybe
born human then things went horribly amiss
then horribly right, the best the gods could do
after fucking you, ripping your arms off
then turning you into a talking snake.
You were after all just wandering a vacant
lot no one told you was sacred, and no one
warned you not to ogle the bathing nymphs
although that you somehow already knew but
couldn't help yourself. Never could you help
yourself, thrashed by seasons of retro snows,
summer tongues, umbrella exploded like a rose,
giddy when the wicked stromboli comes.

Enter Fortinbras

I like to think our lies
are the enduring kind, ones the future
will marvel over from their sustenance tubes

as we marvel now at those batty squiggles
in the desert, the untranslatable pleas
to any number of gods long scared off.

It can't all be trash, can it, mis-
remembered, mishandled, improperly
recycled? The quality of mercy

is not strained, there's like, umm, lumps in it.
No need to get all wussy about the botched
prisms of your negotiations with the darkling

hollyhocks, you're not alone, bucko.
So join me for a lorn nip of some syrupy
aperitif, the last dramatic personae among

the walking stiffs. The slings and thongs
of outrageous fortune, well, no need
to kill yourself over every bomb and extinction.

To be or not to be, what's the big diff?
The kindergarten still rattles away
with kinder until the sun explodes

its finger-painted splotch, covering
the stage with defunct fakers until some yahoo

comes on to say he'll explain everything,
he who doesn't have a clue or far too many.

Psalm

Some of us may find the truth
in the cracked agate heart
of these afternoons by the salutary waters,
striking friezes in the droll clay.
A thing begun by dragon's teeth
sown in dust may end in an airy cocoon
but it is the middle we are muddled in
like a trial convened testimonies ago.
Who were those original plaintiffs anyway?
Because the gods wished to understand poignancy,
they dropped rocks upon us, ground us
in the sidewalk with their immaculate heels,
drove their chariots through our markets
so we might be caught up and turned
into axle grease
when probably a slap in the face would do
or the face on top of the true face
we know is under there somewhere
stitched with neurons like a jellyfish.
Another season has plumped these melons,
hemmed wildflowers in the skullcap, doused
the holding tanks, hatcheries overflowing,
another night muffling the children,
those lambs,
so we are free to spelunk our own wounds
that have grown so glossy and numb,
a feast for metaphor.
But weren't those real arrows
borne in a real eagle's claws,
real people with iffy inner ears,
inebriated libidos who laid out
their paltry wares and saw them turned to gold,
who bathed naked in hidden cataracts,
drank from a single cup that never emptied,
who cried out in dark lichen-flickered passageways
and were answered?

2

Flood Plain

The red jacket waits in the closet to go by.
The lizard waits in the sunshine to go by.
Money, large denominations, waiting to go by.
Youth going by, the heart turns to solder
then no, a mimosa tree. Herd of elk, milk
on the shelf, the kingdom of the elf.
Piñatas going by. Wham, birthday boy
swats, scattering trinkets and sweets.
Flash going by the camera. 500 miles per hour
weekend, speed of light Dalmatian pup.
Great mental effort going by but not enough
to mend a string. In a red jacket, you go by,
the moment lost, firecracker gone off, just
gunpowder-smelling shreds. The day drags by
the moon then the moon returns as if looking
for its keys. On the table they wait
not going anywhere it seems to the naked
eye but actually flying by, flying apart,
made of atoms locked in repulsive force.
My buddy's son now six feet tall, took all
of what? twenty minutes. Stop! Hard not to want
to get a choke-hold on something anything,
a piece of bread, stay, it can't. Spring
throwing itself a parade as it goes by,
fire truck, veterans, jet plane, wedding
going by so long the end's a funeral.
Popsicle stick bumping down rain-glutted
gutter. Let it go, says the wise man,
lest you be too weighed down going
where you must go by.

Desert Ode

When you look into the still, deep water,
you can feel it looking back,
trying to come up with the proper punishment.
Fucking water, who made you the boss?
I like the parts in my brain best
that can look at a puddle of blood
and reach for a mop
although the parts that reach for a paintbrush
have been of equal help.
When I take my orphan brain to the desert
it is especially appreciative of all the glitter,
glitter the result of indiscriminant shatter.
It's the desert! You can throw rocks anywhere!
And each eye is the eye of god
now all deranged.
Whatever She thinks of you going in
isn't what She thinks going out.
You might want to make a sacrifice
and don't expect a sliding scale
or a grade curve.
No one comes out of the desert
a college administrator or realtor,
although you might be able to perform
brain surgery with a stone knife.
In the desert I feel like I'm made
entirely of broccoli.
The joy is surviving the poisonous sunset.
If you are caught with a single to-do list,
you will be executed.
You will be tied to a chair
and you'd better not float.
If you harass a single hallucination,
you will be executed.
Drowning has nothing on the desert
when it comes to striking your head like a match.

Why I was pardoned, I don't know.
I could only name 27 different kinds of sand.
I kept jabbering about meteor showers,
how it depends on your point of view.
It was hard to imagine anyone making
a pornographic movie in the desert
but that just shows how naïve I was.
What did I know about eating a human heart?
You just need really long extension cords.
That's why I thought anyone I met
in the desert was an angel suffering
from amnesia. Either surgery
with a stone knife as the cause or cure.
Don't bother trying to explain though.
They'll forget instantly, like rabbits.
Just offer up your athletic beverage,
maybe that's how you'll be spared.

Liverwurst

My sandwich had not expected such travails
and now it has a story to tell,
another saga of my personal failures
like the upside-down tulip bulbs'
short journey to hell
and the guitar lessons from the casualty
who still had the solo hair
but not the drugs no siree
he'd stop the power chords
to convince himself was not the bust
of a dark sacred task.
Like drawing a perfect hexagon
without the hexagon-drawing tool.
Or swimming a long way underwater,
touching the wall and swimming back.
By then a new argument has taken over your brain
which is becoming a raisin
instead of a crystal palace
where czars and czarinas
are sitting down to a giant swine dinner
and wolves chase troikas on the steppes
and idiots play flag football in the mists.
Go long, one shouts
and it's 30 years later.
The spaceship has lost course
while the crew was in suspended animation.
Now there is an extra being on board, snarling.
I get the feeling I should be somewhere now.
Somewhere else.

Wheelchair Race

You can't understand how everyone else
walks around in flames, how they get through
the vapor locks, the persistent mazes
and partitions between you and the flowers
and the ideals and sprays of life
and goodness exhibits.
It feels like there's a gray box on your head.
It is your head.
Boxhead.
Filled with flakes although some settling has occurred
and a decoder ring to no known code
but you want to be found out.
You leave pink stick 'ems on the portal,
profligate with fingerprints.
You leave a gasp on the hotel pillow.
At least you have the strength of your evictions,
not much really, the abandonment of a mouse,
a couch, a girlfriend, the complete second season on DVD,
all to the plus for a guilt complex,
the technicolor of dreams.
The days of the dollar entrance fee
to the palace of pixie dust are long gone.
The calendar has decided where to set
your death, back in that coal town
with its alleys leading to the river
where you were told you'd always drown,
where your fundamental experience was a hybrid
of boredom and dread you wouldn't get
to the bathroom on time.
No one thought you'd survive
yet one of your hands still glows
from touching the cheek of Apollo
who had disguised himself as Lisa Wolfgang's breast.
Just like in the sixties except
everyone suspected everyone else

of having a personal nuclear device
kept separate from the general bomb
that once promised the comfort of a stalemate.
You befriended a wounded squirrel
but he went on to success in the bureaucracy
that refers to you as occupant.
Boxhead evicted occupant.
If only you had one of those penlights
that's also a penknife,
you could make the air holes bigger
but it's probably best you can't see
what you're cutting apart.
Right now the only place air gets in
is where your mother kissed your head
when it was still soft as mucilage
and she still a shiny dragonfly.

Revolutions Tend toward Orthodoxy

Almost time for the September Massacres.
William Wordsworth is wandering around
impressing the soft wax of his mind
in that 65% oblivious way
of a 24-year-old about to knock up
a counterrevolutionary in spite of
his republican essayistic chops
maybe because of his not-too-hot French
and being inside the brig of a young, male British body.
It's not called English kissing after all.
Previously he's been so moved by a tree,
a ghost story, a vagrant and long walks
but still he's having trouble being born,
the revolutionaries sitting around on sacks
of raw flageolets, progenitors
of the beanbag chair. They are waiting
for Robespierre, regrettably. Later
the trial of Marie Antoinette
makes the poet in his birth canal nervous
even with those champagne glasses
molded from her breasts.
Somehow the Committee of Public Safety
accentuates her beauty, what
the Reign of Terror has in common
with a pushup bra.
Napoleon is getting ready,
he does not see his end in Elba
turning into a dessert.
Edmund Burke is getting ready.
Flower Power is getting ready
(skipping ahead).
The crystal doorknobs are wiped with disinfectant.
The bread is distributed to the battlements.
600 heads in one week.
Outrage, conviction, bliss, dreadful outcome,

hope, disappointment, oh imagination, repeat.
Daffodils are getting ready in their dirt.
The Prelude is getting ready but not until
Wordsworth's death, the dedication removed.

Gawker

You are toilet head.
No, I am toilet head.
You are a moose.
Your hose is a moose's soaker hose.
It goes into the garden.
God's mad, everyone out!
We sniff glue.
I have a medium-sized White House in my sperm.
We can't decide who to sue.
You are not moose actually.
Because your mother wasn't.
Allowances have to be made
like when the new recruits line up
backs to the big-ass light source.
Are they angels or snakes?
Sometimes through their raiment see
to the monogrammed elastic.
Closer, closer.
Things get out of hand.
An affidavit thrown into a bush.
So long ago the bush burns it.
Rain helps digestively.
A redwing blackbird dies.
No one will forget.
No, did and shouldn't.
But back to you, the no longer moose.
How does it feel to be the biggest marsupial in North America?
Like you're about to be killed?
Would your sister's vaginal opening welcome me?
Not that I'm asking.
For a talking non-moose, you don't say much.
I like that in chairs too.
Everyone else is a fucking liar.
Look at their root-hairs,
their briefcase full of yum-yums.

But here is a parking sticker.
It makes you an emeritus.
There is so much to love in this world
I forgive you for feeling you're about to die.
I cannot be your golden bra.
Let's get drunk and break stuff against each other.
Tiny African gods fall out.
Let's form insignia.
People will think we've been to war together.
Parts of the map will make us sniffle.
Parades will make us moan.
A moan is the moon pulling something out of you.
You owe the moon a lot.
Payback time.
Look at the sea, moaning.
Have a havoc.
Now is the time for our evacuation.
I mean vacation.
The big dictionary is our Grand Guignol.
I am feeling interstitial.
Let's catch up on our correspondence.
Simplicity of structure and lucidity of phrase
permit a vastly disparate tonal array.
Or something.
What other explanation for the rainbow?
Forgiveness is the puppy in our parlor.
Here comes the snow.
Would that it would never end.

From the Get-Go

On the eighth day me and Fucking Dickhead
running along the forest, stipulating Hey!
trying to sort things out, the turtles
lying with the mothers of invention,
the quadratic equation still inside the mouse
Hey! night and day mixing it up, probably
as straight as they'll ever get, one's the gum
in the other's hair. Undropsical butterflies
perplex the wildebeest's wound, angels
constipated with diamonds. Can't be helped,
sings Fucking Dickhead, never one to miss
a scripture on a skull, a dull knife's handi-
work, the boulder in the eye of the beholder.
See this fleur-de-lis throw? Verily, even the softest
pillow can muffle a scream. Look right look left
uphill down, you're still roadkill. Fuckhead,
says I for short, what a floor plan and not half
the blueprint unrolled but ain't there a more
favorable riverboat, higher crap odds? I see
glaciers breaking like ice trays, some mighty
aggrieved elephants, cheesy special effects. I see
France, I see your underpants. You was expecting
crystal pj's? An all-night flight to paradise,
free bottomless mixed nuts? You want a balanced
checkbook, get off the teeter-tot. Okay then,
giddyup, fast forward duking it out with
flashback, voiceover going down on
the understory. Tyger, tyger, says Dickhead
which he always says when he gets another idea:
cling wrap, smart bomb, mechanical bull,
and because he's half god, half cartoon,
Fuckhead keeps blowing himself up and putting
himself back together wrong, just don't be the one
breaking his fall which is why, of course,
you're here in your porcelain crowns, gorged

on viol concertos and rot-gut, night beaded
with dog bark, why you've washed up in this town
of burnt-out pyros and photo-sensitive surfer chicks,
a big lab where they're figuring out how much
a creature can live without a head. I'm betting
lots. Somewhere under the rainbow, the old war
between figuration and abstraction settles
on the landscape, extremer dramaturgies
possessing some swifts building nests
of dental floss. Does the heart good to see
our refuse thus employed. It's late but not
as late as it was before we watched you fall
for a tombstone-filching off-his-meds young gun
and when you bailed him out and sat in the Pancake House,
you took his theories into your Tuileries,
his message onto your machine until the queen
believed it and turned against herself and the king
believed it and turned against himself.
Now that you're big enough,
you can set fire to whatever you want,
eat burning ice cream, drink burning Schnapps,
even the mayor's loudspeaker truck gives way,
even the Herr Doktor's death-mobile.
Don't you love what we've done with artificial organs?
Don't you love waiting in emergency rooms?
Washing your hands with that pink soap
greasy as gun oil? Don't you love
filling out the forms in triplicate, watching
the owls until it's too dark to tell
what they're tearing apart?
This world was made for you.

Admissions Policy

We thought we might be able to close
the school for people with pieces missing
for the summer but no one would graduate,
they wouldn't put on their black capes
and throw their mortarboards in the air.
More and more kept showing up, partially,
obviously worthy of admission. One
of our most promising freshmen didn't have a skull,
his brains held together by, you guessed it,
duct tape. Duct tape occupies a significant
portion of our curriculum in the school
for people with pieces missing
as does reading original poetry aloud
and being rewarded with grapes.
Often students are given exercises
like imagining they're broken canyon birds
or not using the letter I
or holding your breath until you pass out
then writing rapidly as you regain consciousness.
It's all about coming back.
Some students appear intact
but have supped on the pomegranate seeds of Dis
to speak mythologically,
and they never come the whole way back.
Their color is wrong
like grass under a tarp.
Sure, they use cutlery without incident,
they don't need special vaults to compete
but they're the most rewarding pupils
even if they have to be told repeatedly
their dog died long ago,
the ones who think they can fly
because they have no shadow,
who never get old
and just keep sitting there after the barkeep

turns on the harsh everyone-out overheads,
their last call empty of all
but a slurry of ice, paper umbrella,
plastic sword. Try being a ghost of yourself
then tell me your mind burns
for no reason,
tell me the world is radioactive
for no reason.
Why else would you come here
so dangerously without your space helmet,
so recklessly afield with the coyotes,
looking for bluets for your wreath?

Sex with Strangers

I was having sex with a stranger
when I realized this was no stranger,
this was Eleanor Roosevelt,
wife of the 32nd president of the United States.
Of course I was shocked
but it seemed rude to stop having sex
so I went on having sex.
Her hair was getting rather deranged
and she was concentrating hard
like a person trying to move a paperclip
by force of mind alone
which brought out the equine qualities
of her facial structure not in a bad way.
One reason to have sex is to help a stranger
get in touch with his or her animal being
even if it's a crayfish.
In the kitchen the rotisserie was laboring,
either the chicken was too fat
or it was tuckering out. Oddly,
I didn't feel bad for Franklin Delano
even though he looked jaunty and vulnerable
in his wheelchair in the margin of the dictionary.
In general it's difficult to feel bad
about anything while having sex
which is why it's such a popular activity
and the church is against it
except in rare primarily utilitarian instances.
That pretty much covers the facts of my life.
I've never been in much of a car crash.
When I walk into the mirror of the high grass
under the tired suicide note of the setting sun,
I'm never gone long. Once I was stuck
on an elevator, all of us strangers
gasping at once but there the resemblance
to having sex ended because it only took

35 seconds to get going again, each of us
off at a different floor: cardiology,
oncology, psychiatry, the burn unit,
the solarium.

Poem on a Theme by Tony Hoagland

I have a big erection.
Most mythology goes into it.
Destroyer god with one thousand arms
and ceintures of skulls.
Gigantic traumatic swan.
I'm sure glad I'm not trying to pass through airport security
with this big erection.
Those of you who also have erections
may call them big
but you are misusing the word.
I suppose I could run after a thief if I had to,
I could probably do some math problems if I must
but having a big erection
makes you feel there's not much else you have to do
except use the big erection!
The uses of which vary from
the creation of civilization (figurative)
to intercourse (literal) with the harmonic half of a sister act.
In the middle is Picasso's oeuvre
excluding the sissy Blue Period.
Also it must be admitted
some pretty messed-up behavior
which is the foundation of many video games
society deserves to be alarmed about
but I submit this is more the result
of the suppression of the erection's beauteous expression
by the uptight
than any specifically inherent evils.
Indeed, an erection, if not usually a sign of pacifism,
neither is it necessarily an indication of murderous rage.
Some ducks have bigger penises than gorillas after all.
So if you want to campaign against testing cosmetics on laboratory
    animals,
don't ask a big erection.
But knocking down a wall? You bet!

Maybe there's a garden out there worth a look-see.
Hey, there's a woodpecker in a tree.
Nature had prepared this avian visitor
for its head-banging activity
by installing gaskets and cushions and hammocks in its skull
to avoid brain damage.
Wow, look at that little pecker go!
A divine providence provides for us all.

Force of Rabbit

Haven't you learned a thing?
Here is a cube, you have 30 seconds.
Put it down now and slowly back away,
gather what ye may in a paper sack,
we must bulldozer your house,
says right here in the denouement,
your birth certificate.
Lump it.
Lick it and die.
Your mother sold you out.
Your dentist sold you out.
Bases loaded, you popped out.
No, this stain will never come out.
Over and out.
Remember that incident with the finger-paint?
It wasn't finger-paint.
It may not look like this tiny bunny
could have much force
but it is being implanted in your brain.
Remember the dented girl you made cry?
She's now entirely titanium, dotted with flashbulbs.
She's 100 feet tall and looking for you.
She wants to forgive you.
She wants you to be her egg.
You're dew.
So you ask her to coffee
wrong move
like asking a flamethrower to a forest fire
so try a turkey dinner
might calm you down
and many other occasions even shopping
for moccasins for sneaking
then you put your hand upon her unexploding
anti-narcolysing summer boulevard breast,
meet no noncompliance ergo to bed

dot dot dot exclamation
then watch her take a shower. Survive!
Survive her fennel muffins and her boredom
re: your rabbity ideas then slowly
approach her using all you know
of spiders' mating practices, thrumming
the web, stroking her high-voltage head
then grasping the marry-me knob. She does.
The ceremony is by some crazy water.
Approximately 80% of the guests are nonhuman.
Her sister has a hatchet in her forehead
it seems rude to mention. Do you have any
mental illness in your family
too late to ask. Your brother
is in a bathysphere. You sell
your comic book collection
to buy her a rose arbor. She
gives you a power tool. You go
to her mother's grave and the deer
eating its flowers says something
that makes her cry in a good way
like rain on a sunny day. She is
the most delicate thing in the world,
don't ruin her. Wham, crash, still
she's unruined. Suddenly
you're one thousand years old.
Your knee is made of snow.
Still you're trying to see through her clothes.
Still she's happy to see you.
Somehow you haven't fucked everything up,
you didn't paint the lane lines
straight into a tree. A veteran
gives you a triumphant refrigerator magnet.
A parking meter in a plastic bag
looks like the head of a Roman emperor.
You grow out of your jumpsuit.
You inhale fibers from a fake beard
and cough up blood theatrically.

The committee decides to preserve
your anarchic spelling.
She did not let you become a gorilla
throwing an orange bucket in despair.
You hope she didn't feel alone.
Now you lie peaceful in her ocean air,
not even bothering to fox the page,
sleep a blue parallelogram,
tomorrow an umbrella planted in sand.
A small rocket takes off for a distant star.
A creature crawls from the swamp, mewing.
Mrs. Crampton calls the children in to lunch
even though they are all quite grown
and no longer in the country.

Briar

After the final battle of the gods,
the rain tasted like iron forever.
And after forever, the worst was over
until another worst volunteered.
Not to say green tips didn't thrust
from mordent roots or nests
percolate with starlings.
Even the cockroach sports
vertiginous wings.
Pilgrim, what the fuck . . . ?
No one knows if the chunk of ice
in the center of the chest
was part of a planet of ice
before we began
so full of impurities,
it could be flint,
it could be a soul,
each of us chipped off.
Three or four lifetimes later,
I hope I'm not the same drunkard
although the enemies are the same,
galloping against each other
over the boneyards of horses,
blowing the pump houses,
torching the bell towers.
Three children beating
an already injured snake
make a civilization.
Agony is an art like any other
and deserves to be forgotten.
Imagination is the vacation
of meaning, thinks the snake,
the earth's other minions
come to dispose of the remains,
spine to summer hearth,
spine to winter castle.

Then the businessmen arrive
messaging the invisible
so some of us flee with our white wine.
You don't want to be around me now.
What isn't born twisted?
Even the lily leaf, the hummingbird.
There was a man who couldn't
straighten and he fell from nowhere.
Ask him and he'll say he was elected
into the new order, new orchard
where fruit can't rot or ripen.
For a sum, a mechanism
produces your future.
Can the mind function without
its scorpion? Scorpion warmed
in a corner, allowed its repose.
The ocean rubs its belly,
come sleep with me,
the surface hugely scratched,
jagged like illustrations of electricity,
thinks the woman on the porch
who in three days must move her mother
into a bottle of antiseptic
because she's leaving the oven on.
Obscene abbreviations.
When the man comes out, clinking
his ice, she has already turned
into six or seven other people,
each with a necklace of tiny skulls,
a strange power, a debt.
The snake was already dead
by anyone's account.
It was a small thing getting smaller.
It was the animal you were
before the animal you've become.
A boy has found a bullet
by the swing-set.
Something's written on it.

3

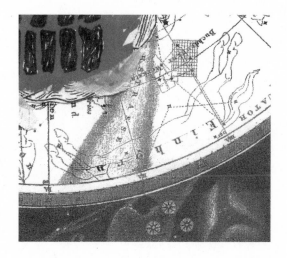

You

That wasn't your head rolling by, was it?
You haven't gone off your meds again, have you?
For the halos in the morning, nooses by afternoon.
Elegant are the pajamas for the voyage,
nailed the shingles to the house.
I'll never forget when I touched your breast
you sighed a name proximate my own.
I wasn't a tree or a cloud or a crow.
We both had someplace else to go, leaning
over other railings, letting the sea have the letter.
I'm sorry I kicked you apart then reassembled
you wrong, always an extra piece or two
because it seemed the right thing to do
to replace your brain with a fuse box,
your voice with a stereo so under my pillow
the subwoofer could go, little purr,
little wolf, let's eat each other's hearts.

Learning to Live with Bliss

Kissing a rose is a dumb thing to do
not just from the rose's point of view.
But it's a start
like driving off a cliff's probably a finish.
In between you'll want to go to Mexico,
get so drunk you think what you're doing is a dance.
Remember though, tattoo removal is costly, painful
and depending on your insurance
they might use a sharpened stone.
Wondrous is the matter of this temporary world.
Regard the twists of the bugle
that yield one clear clarion.
Regard the neuron's long run
from spine to pinkie's tip.
Because all atoms are mostly empty space,
theoretically it's possible
to pass a machete through your brain
without disturbing a nap's dream
if you proceed slowly enough,
it's like one vacuum passing through another
except for some infinitesimal nudging,
infinitesimal excuse me's,
but who has time for that?
The car you drove off the cliff?
In a jiff, it's headed toward the water
that gets pretty noncompliant when bitch-slapped.
It ain't a rose that goes all loves me loves me not.
But you know what I like?
Retablos, those testimonies of miracles
crudely painted on sheet metal
and little skeleton figurines
all dressed up, bride and groom, bone dog.
And TV trucks by the crash site with 15-foot antennae
looking like they'd be easy to tip over

and who doesn't like tipping stuff over?
See those tots stacking blocks
just so they can knock them down?
They're in training.
They're working up to kissing a rose.

Triage

Fatally, the boy picks up a what he thought
on the occupier/insurgent fractioned
road. Fatally, the man goes out for popsicles
in the storm not for himself for his two
days later from the mudslide pulled he's
given a kind of super power, drive a nail
into his chest he won't care or notice.
The deluge greens the hills, the world
is full of wailing, concussions, unnerved
stillness, hushed discussion, then more
wailing but a birdsong still fits through
two quick notes sailing then what to do
how what needs stopping stop, speed what
needs now not? Check trickling through
the mail, joining an envelope-gush fed
into a machine that slits them open
counting. Groups of same-thinkers praying
which seems okay unless you study history
where such behavior's often preparatory
to raving, attack, more slaughter. Somehow
a bicyclist fits through, bell on handlebars.
Then mother comes home, syntax stays intact,
a lie begins to wither. The man can't fit
through barbed wire but his poems do, hidden
in his breath. Laughter fitting through at first
seems monstrous. "She'd be your age by now."
Time fitting through a fruit tree, an owl.
A string quartet of kids, a room with a
chocolate on the pillow. Outside, an un-
frozen river for those still alive.

Fire Ode

What gift is this the day forces
upon the hapless tangerine tree?
It is the gift of sunlight for chlorophyll
to do what it will in the continuing
nourishment of the tree and me
who its fruit is chewed by, swallowed
mixed with digestive juices and ransacked
for fuel just as the fire ransacks air
for oxygen to bind gasses to, what
it frees from the thoughtless-looking
wood. Behind, it leaves a heap
of smudgy stuff lesser than a dream
that can not be recalled. Of what
was once a house, a lawn or limb
or nearly anything fire fancies.
Oh, what fun to quaff the ignited
tequila shot and la la feel hot
flame-o all things revealed
burning with their secret being
like a frog-pond with frogs, obviously
the pianist, not so much the cinder block
but it too runs a temperature, fever of itself.
So praise the flicker and the power
even though it abbreviates us ash.
Better to dash than never go at all,
the error is not to fall but to fall
from no height. Or so's the argument
of Andrew Marvel as long as his poem lasts.
Which turns out could be forever although
coy mistress and himself long cinder and dust be.
Either that or rust like a busted tractor
abandoned in a snowy field now suitable
for only artsy photographs that speak
of loneliness and passion spent
as well as peaceable, elegant resignation
which makes me want to scream.

Ash Ode

When I saw you ahead I ran two blocks
shouting your name then realizing it wasn't
you but some alarmed pretender, I went on
running, shouting now into the sky,
continuing your fame and luster. Since I've
been incinerated, I've oft returned to this thought,
that all things loved are pursued and never caught,
even as you slept beside me you were flying off.
At least what's never had can't be lost, the sieve
of self stuck with just some larger chunks, jawbone,
wedding ring, a single repeated dream,
a lullaby in every elegy, descriptions
of the sea written in the desert, your broken
umbrella, me claiming I could fix it.

Lots of Questions

How strange to arrive anywhere.
Then what? Turn on the hotel room TV
to check for a good storm, find some water
to walk on, partake of the local produce,
size up the local pearls? And how do
the indigenous sleep in this din? Wrapped
in their wings hanging upside-down
or woven in piles, perpetrating
a collective snore? Is this where god
fits in with lots of reading matter
and antimatter? Someone who knows
better says it's all a joke but he who
knows the most thinks it's the only way
to fly an egg, his authority based
on years of pubic service. At which point
I tugged off the headphones and turned from
that ambience of mispronounced
misprint to the more immediate
miracles, scrape of chairs, jackhammers'
retorts, some squalling babe
with a bumped head being taken out.
Is this the proof god's been looking for
that we exist, what makes up this world
we are in flight from, amniotic
chimeras of the past tearing at
the shrink-wrapped future?
Don't try to tell me it'll all work out,
that a blind tinkerer always comes up
with an answer just as the sun comes up
to put a tooth-pasty gleam
on the mess of last night.
I still feel a little woozy drunk
but mostly I was hardly there
which means not much here either.

Earth Science Lab Partner

How little it all amounts to.
So take comfort, you're just a blip,
an anomaly, datum to be discarded,
negligible as a chorus member with the sniffles,

your totem animal a baloney sandwich,
your life dismissed without a trial,
so stay awhile, whatever burns inside you,
face come back from childhood in a dream,

the humiliations, split seams, lies, dumb
disguises, underachieved overreaches
are nothing beyond the ken of a crayfish,
nothing a rock's not suffered,

one among billions, chipped off,
dragged through the desert, aberrant,
once miles under water with a head still
full of kelp, wherever you are,

you don't belong but don't worry,
you won't be there long even if
it'll feel like eternity, your carry-on
ransacked, mashing your snack,

or in line at the DMV reading Coleridge,
or in the cardiologist's foyer
with its cheery cheesy sunrise art
and Tiresias breathing through a tube

telling your fortune from a trapped fly.
You're the part that breaks off first
and makes no difference, the churning goes on
in the slaughterhouse, the ice polished at the rink,

the shadows doing their rabbit act
while you're at the sink. It's not that hard,
is it, to become one of them? Remember
trying a weightless walk on the beach to see

if you could leave the sand without a mark?
You played trumpet in the high school marching band
and half the time didn't bother blowing.
The first girl who let you touch her breast

was killed by a drunk driver. Your mouse's
name was Mystic and he lived three years.

Private Waterfall

You must be careful eating thorns
not to eat the maudlin fruit.
I find it completely impossible to fear my death
when I'm nauseous
so planes in turbulence, boats in high seas—
no problemo.
But spring drizzle,
a bird mispronouncing my name,
I dive for the shadows
that only have a passing relationship
to what casts them.
Oh no they don't, little chirrup,
it is shadows that cast the material world.
So okay, maybe they slept together once
when one was very sad and drunk.
You have to be very careful
when you're sad and drunk
and the river wants you to star in its cabaret
and the artificial flavor factory is concentrating on almond.
You have to be careful
when you're absently tearing apart a plastic cup
that when you move on to yourself
it's easier, deckles at the edges
like expensive handmade paper
on which you feel mighty hesitant writing a thing.
Or you could use little scissors to make snowflakes
or a line of deformities holding hands.
I know you were punished when you were young
and that punishment took more and more complex forms
like a single-celled slap in the face
becoming mammalian humiliation
by the same force that led you from finger-painting
to tax evasion.
But remember how it felt to paint a flower,

how a flower was the basic building block of all things:
a hand, a house, a horse, the sun,
mommy, daddy, baby, you,
a bandage, a valentine, a flame.
It still is.

Lives of the Primitives

Shouldn't someone have run for help by now?
When I was a child someone was always running for help.
None returned

but I still like to think of them snookered in phlox,
sucking on a hookah, getting the lowdown from the giant worm.
Everyone was wiser then, knew better,
the same force at work in the campfire
as the apocalypse, no one was excluded

except those who disqualified themselves
by being poor and dirty, not speaking proper English,
low scores, fidgeting during naptime, the deranged.
I knew I was one of them
or would be soon enough
once my sinecure gave out

and I'd crash among the pickpockets and divorcees,
dictionary readers, addicts of the instant,
kids with stigmata and spectacular tits,
intemperate artistic folk
counterfeiting wounds for a public
that could never hurt enough.
Obviously, I'm damaged goods,

even in my three-piece some kind of dictum
from the ant world eats at my nonchalance.
Sure I'd left some broken hearts behind
I don't mind saying and won't be getting
any refunds soon. A new pod of recruits
paces off the wrestling rink, Harvard is in the air.
There's so much we still don't know:

the life expectancy of a squirrel, the lair
of the giant squid, the monetary systems
of those vanished tribes. How strange

to be among westerners again, no longer
handcuffed and strapped in plastic in the driving snows
of the second higher pass, a failed performance
I admit, not like my pal who painted everything

red. Red of swallowed shout,
red of pig's snout, he had some kind of argument
and went on to make a mill and kill himself
then really rake it in. Funny to read
what they write about him now

as if the whole thing wasn't an accident,
the radio on comic opera, the sewage
singing to the sea, the sea swinging back,
as if he wasn't someone who loved a joke
especially on himself.

Pelt

Everyone gets a hurricane name,
a moon drunk in a puddle.
A repaired toy, well almost.
Will the world of bee-bored fruit
ever return to sting our lips?
God some kind of rhinoceros.
A word too is a hole of fire.
The vroom vroom of the refrigerator.
The cold hand of death from the TV set.
The owl I saw in the outlet parking lot,
did it survive the news crawl?
To what world do I belong hey ho?
Was I the pelt mashed in the road,
a carillon in the sleeping room?
Hundreds of faces of smoke hey ho.
15 bucks for plasma.
Why did I come with only a plum?
Why did I leave at a run?
Once I saw a snake with a snake in its mouth.
Some kind of swamp.
The call from the White House to enlist.
Some kind of bigger toxic swamp.
I saw my father tearing something to bits.
I saw couples kissing at the dock,
red X's where they'd be shot.
The plot, the counterplot.
I drank in cancellation.
What broke so easily was already broke?
I saw trees choke.
I felt so guilty I could not move.
I felt so angry I could not move
but if I was invited to tea with Laura Bush
I'd go and break and take whatever I could.
I'd make them have to throw me out,
fight as if it was my own house
overrun by thugs and liars and thieves.

Lives of the Orphans

I am not a flower.
I am a chunk of meat
sprayed by the department store cosmetic technicians,
their mystique something musky
a long way from its pig-drool source.
Who can say I am not
a chunk of meat left over from the last kings of earth,
the only chunk of meat not eaten by flowers
in the terrible triumph of flowers?
Who can find my signet decoding ring?
Who can sell my teeth to the teeth museum?
I was small, sitting in a tree eating mulberries.
My fantastic instruction was just beginning.
When it rained I practiced drawing triangles.
I invented heaven for the pussy.
I invented hell for the cocaine.
Of course I was sent away
to spend my hours talking to birds
instead of carrying a gun on stage
announcing a change in the winds.
Finally I got an iguana.
When I made love I shouted the names of Greek warships.
I was asked to stop that.
To join the debate of the beautiful suicides,
I tried to become a pure white cube
but not sugar, definitely not sugar.
The headlights passed through our hotel room,
their mythical beasts alive for an instant only.
What could I slay that wasn't the same chunk of meat as me?
I watched the gutter overflowing saying, I am your mother.
No you're not.
My real mother burst into flame
smoking a Chesterfield in a paper shift.
White was the fire, white was her shift.
Seeing the hatchet in my heart she said,

How do you think that makes me feel?
Everything has a cause
and a curse
and a tiny face in a locket,
the horn-blower.

Sparkler

I spend the day trying to elude my shadow.
Now it's waiting for me to surface.
It's eaten nothing a gull wouldn't eat
starting with the eyes, always that jelly.

There's a tiny baby in there, breathing
like a frogman. The shadow isn't bothered
by the squirming of what it swallows,
it doesn't have to be turned upside-down 24 times a day
like the mind does because it's an hourglass.

Like someone who's finished the test first,
it acts superior while you're still trying
to decipher the cheat code on the bottom
of your sneaker. I have stayed under
as long as I can. The red vault in my head
opens wider. Shadow, your ringtone's too pretty to answer,

when you were little you never had to worry
about being tied to a chair. It was how

they said they'd find out the truth.
You never had to worry about the truth
or the chair or the red vault in your head
as you tried to stay under longer and longer.
Hello, you just wore your garlands.

You made love to buildings.
You leaned your ladder against Nijinsky.
The flame that comes out of the top of my head

is burning down through my neck.
I wasn't going to be all right.
They intended a sacrifice all along,
scented me so beetles would finish the job.
My shadow will have to find another way home.

An Orgasm Is a Spaceship

Just as it is difficult
to imagine pounding a nail
into every peach in the orchard,
so too it is difficult to imagine
a situation that couldn't be improved
by an orgasm.
Let's go pick some green beans.
Let's buff us some hubcap.
Have you ever run after someone,
holding out a dropped fuzzy glove?
Or say you're in a hotel room in the nation's capital
worrying about the Joint Chiefs of Staff,
who the fuck do they think they are?
when a wee mouse of oh oh oh
comes through the wall.
Out-of-body-experience!
A butterfly in a hypodermic needle!
Doesn't just the sigh of a bubble bath
make you happy?
Even if it's not yours.
Even if you're looking at it through your cage bars
and all you have to play with
is an empty bleach jug.
But back to the spaceship.
All those hours of expectation,
lots of sit-ups.
What will it be like to escape the earth's gravitational field?
Will it hurt much?
The T-minus dot dot dot kaBOOM!
No wonder your brains are all over the ceiling.
Wait, no they're not,
they're right where they've always been.
In the jaws of an alligator.

Our Kind of People

About 50% of my people
were conceived by fornicating drunks.
If they didn't start that way,
that's how they ended up
and the other half the opposite.
And screw you if you think this is about alcohol,
as if your heart isn't a polis of bees,
as if you too haven't staggered through the gloxinia.
One was hospitalized
for inhaling the fibers of a fake beard
made of carpet remnants.
Another walked all night with a broken femur
because her masculinity had been insulted.
One pirouetted 50 times chasing his other sleeve.
Many lived on a sheet of ice.
Many green bugs hatched too soon,
became a brief paste.
The new moon's facing away from you,
facing inward and pocked,
and still you can see what life is like
in outer space without an atmosphere.
Your father the tombstone salesman,
your mother the fire director.
Some glisten like hot dogs when they cry,
some like new credit cards,
envelopes proclaiming you qualify!
Confess some lowness, some theft,
who you fucked in the graveyard,
how you're probably nothing but a fake,
they won't rat you out,
they'll probably forget,
concentrating on a flap of skin
pizza-scalded loose on the roof of their mouth.
One just trying not to destroy a muffin
un-skirting it. Animal macro-urge

in an angel suit. One stares all day
at the canvas and the work is throwing the brush down.
One with a dream journal besotted with tears,
one chewing a doll limb in a muddy yard.
The blood is fake but the bleeding's real.
One still trying to call back
that infant joy in the tub.
One a black dot beside a G clef.
One with a box of pet ash.
When they open the suitcase back in the city,
the ocean's still in their clothes.
Bubbles pricking the surface less and less,
bulbs coming up on the graves.
Somehow the tornado turns aside, the house saved.
Somehow they find each other
in the evacuation shelter,
they find each other at the dance.
Two people driving opposite directions
stopping to move a turtle off the road.

My Itty Void

I'll never understand the sublime
the possibility that it's someone lying
facedown in the rain dream I almost
remember reading hundreds of years
all those landscapes' partial collapse
that can only be entered in a mirror
the viewer in the corner alone dwarfed
facing out to sea the possibility it's all
vexation in the pristine undernothing
minor flaws faltering not at ease precisely
but leaning leaning into an eventually
broken like a line in poetry breaks
from sense and sublimates a cloud crosses
the sun and stays last button buttoned
only the explorer's journals remain a few
flowers pressed and unnamed it's not that
no one sees it coming no one sees it coming
and tells everyone you show me mine
I'll show you yours the trumpet goes up
to the lion's mouth but not yet the fog
obscures the other side of the bridge
maybe obscurity is the other side denial
seeping out of the abandonment but
something else hindering the heart lagging
voices coming from the warm cottage behind
the light-source fading the stumps rotted
softened with moss not much further now.

Procession

They're carrying toward you now
the single yellow flower.
They're carrying toward you
the lamb that has been slain.
You with your car keys
on a chain with a toy whistle,
the silver traveler's cup.
Soon you're going 30 mph
through slush and they're hardly moving,
barefoot but they're catching up.
Maybe Saturday, maybe Sunday
when you're entering withdrawals in the checkbook
or sorting the brown glass from the green
into the magnificent bins.
Sometimes you hear singing
in a language you don't know.
You stand in a stone carving,
your hand on the head of a winged cat.
Time to check the smoke alarm.
Isn't that the snow calling you?
Doesn't the bell ring first inside you
then go searching elsewhere?
How did you get to be so hollow
when you came into this world dense
as a ball bearing? You had a black star
sequined to your cap. You learned
just to brush the crumbs from your lap,
to staple the paper plane on the fuselage
the best place for long, straight flight.
Now you're checking a single bag.
The person beside you in the exit row
reads a book with nothing in it.
The captain interrupts the movie
about a comic becoming president
to tell you the name of a river

frozen thousands of feet below.
Remember when you pretended
you came back after so long gone,
pretended the story of the pack of dogs
in the graveyard could end any way?
Whatever snagged in your eye
stopped the world but now nothing
stops the world. Its tires spin
in the alley, its newspaper
thwamps against the door. All the scrapes
and scratches and ripping of paper,
still you're not wholly erased.
There's your cup in the sink.
Your face in the mirror in a circle
of wiped-away fog. It's only
Wednesday, early February
but there's a yellow flower in your cough.

Half Story Half-Life

Alas, we'll never know how it turns out,
if that boy chewing his sock will ever
be diagnosed and welcomed back or the monster
understood at last and killed. We had to turn
the TV off and try to get some sleep, slippery
goddess who never comes when called and then
won't go away. Hard to know what to sacrifice,
what obeisance make. Torch some feverfew?
Dance until the brain floats to the deep end
of the stew or sit at glacial remove
scoring a tablet with po-mo insect song?
Fellow initiates, brother bozo, sister scar,
let us share the paint strips of our hearts,
leadbelly blues, Inverness grays, scab red.
Not that I expect to understand you better
than you do me or less, your addled broken
bike bell, my hostage knock. It's just
that we're together not much longer
and what a relief. Look who's here with us,
Myrtle back from confessional surgery,
Captain Mike with his topical bilge,
the commando, the shampoo salesman,
the reluctant soprano who refuses to sing
unless we plead, cajole, insist, promise
to make fools of ourselves too, forget
ourselves as others are obliged to do
so the world may be restored a portion
of its emptiness and peace.

The Hour Light Streams through the House

Nothing is itself the whole way through,
pass your sword into the fog, you'll hear
metal clink on metal. Even the lofty
personages wrapped in furs have the insides
of seashores. Your glacier became a glacier
because something happened then it wanted
to be alone. The berry thinks it's different
from the thorns it grows among but the seed
knows better. After a while the dead brother's
voice takes up residence in your own. A slight
rearrangement of powders changes everything.
You didn't know how things got so tilted.
It doesn't matter whether I'm here or not.

Scatteration

The feeling of escape keeps eluding me
even while lunching with antelope
gathered round a misfire. I guess
I'm weeping the benefits of my awards,
pockets full of coins like someone intends
to sink me, like I couldn't do that myself.
But let us forget any further recommendations
of the tragicomic self-snuff ilk,
a genre invented for high school productions
of Romeo and co., there's already libraries full,
poor cataloguers never coming up for air.
Not making much headway up here either,
same pasty fingerfood for blood donors,
same glass skulls prohibitively priced,
elopements off cliffs. When my mother dies,
I'm afraid I'll have to return to my hometown,
find it recognizable as someone else's
set design of my bad dreams, humiliations
intact, fresh as cheese, my friends still
haunting me with their superior models
and I still won't know what to do
with the ashes of my dead cat.

Acorn Hitting a Tin Roof

What little difference one death makes.
You go to a different grocery store for a month.
The old one doesn't close. Who can tell
if there's more avocados so ripe
they're half price? It's not like the comet
more people saw in the paper than the sky.
You had to get up before dawn
and the weather had to be right.
One father built it up too much
so his son had to work on disappointment.
After his mother died and his father
had lived alone for a while,
they went to see the Lipizzaners.
How silly to be made to weep
by a horse hopping backward on only its hind legs.
Don't worry, only your father will know
and he'll never tell anyone.

The Pure Intention of the Hornet

The first time I saw my father after he died,
he kept knocking against the window
even though I was afraid
the cat would kill him. At least crash-

landing on the sill then knocking more
was an improvement over the mechanical
bed, no glasses, no teeth, only Holy
shit I'm dying on repeat in his mind,

his three terrified, disgusted, bored offspring
in the ozone waiting room politely ignoring
the bilge from the grief counselor.
They'd had bad dreams before but weren't sure

they too were cinders shooting through the cosmos
from one oblivion to another.
One thought of his convertible in the parking lot,
was it locked? One discarded baby names on her list.

One became an anvil but if you asked,
No, he'd say, he wasn't hurting anyone.
Something green hustled by whose only job
was swabbing surgery floors so it was good

Dad's spirit didn't cling to him, it needed
some air. How can I remember a voice
so clearly but not a thing it said?
The shrinking was immediate. Once

I thought a frog in a puddle in North
Carolina, easy to hold in my hand,
possible to protect. I was wrong.
Then after the fawn coming pickpocket close,

he gave up for years until yesterday's
black stone on the beach with his gentle eye
for which I'm grateful still, and cherish
then heave back into the sea's honeysuckle.

Today They Will Show Me the Homunculus

I knew it was on the other side of the door
gurgling like a leak, still mushy
and wrinkled and pupating, pumping
lymph into its wings.
They'd given me one of its blankies
to try to get me used to it
but I didn't want to be superceded and destroyed.
I didn't want to use such grandiose words,
I knew I had a small place in the leaf litter
processing leaf litter
but I didn't want its spit on my idols.
Whenever they lectured me about trying to try
my quills would stand up
so they'd point to the chain
attached to the washline outside,
churned up mud beneath,
an empty bleach jug to play with.
Had they forgotten how crazy with happiness
they were when I nose-bounced the orange ball,
when I brought home papers stickered with stars,
how I got promoted at the pyramid?
Since the arrival of the homunculus
they couldn't sleep, they'd neglect to light
the incense in the shrine, he hadn't
mounted her for weeks, they'd forgotten
my birthday, their eight eyes grown
cloudy, their bridal webs weighed down
with dust. Soon I too will be weighed down
with dust in an ordinary way, at a chair
that's comfortable but too low,
even the napkin folded under the table leg
not stopping the wobbling.
Or trotting by the paralyzed fireman's house
with the pinwheels in the kale garden
or the house of the disgraced politician

with the blinds never closed
or the graveyard where the children play tag
and my rudimentary heart will give out
and I know the homunculus will be there,
adjusting the oxygen mask then deciding
to turn off the machines, pressing my paws
and skull into the tar-pit for preservation,
swearing to remember, swearing
there will never be another like me, making sure.

Like My Older Sister

I too wanted the aliens to return
to finish what they started probably
by accident but that didn't mean
lying on the roof like one of god's cheating

cheerleaders or shock therapy for a year
because she couldn't get the drill straight,
messing up halftime and they caught her
at the train station with red luggage

she bought with the stolen magazine money
and she kicked out the back car window.
This was the sixties, I was still fascinated
by how safety glass shattered—preciously,

and she hardly had to bother getting pregnant
to get a miniature vacuum cleaner
shoved up in her in Puerto Rico
where it was legal. When she came back

without a single skyrocket or seashell
and our mother began dipping artificial flowers
in gold paint in the basement,
the take-me-to-your-leader sign

didn't even make her laugh.
I guess she'd been to see the leader
and it wasn't some glow-in-the-dark
empathetic sunflower with antennae

who had a plan for world vegetarianism
and the end of the war.
It was something that smelled like asphalt,
that could hardly get out of bed,

nothing that could make nonthreatening
replies to birds, something whose teeth
weren't even real. But devouring
doesn't necessarily mean chewing

and swallowing what's torn from the bone.
Some things only need a wound to feed.

Blue Limbo

I couldn't tell the snowflake that foretells
my death from the other lunkhead flakes
that couldn't scare a chicken, dandruffy
weak blips in the big what huh,
cell phones swallowed by sharks,
music that freezes the violinist,
a conversation with dirt.
It never works out neatly enough,
our trouble with the flux, calculating
luminosity. Sooner or later, I'll reach up
and my ruby will be gone, perhaps
in the aquarium hour of squishing
in the vat of our own desuetude,
oenophiles of lost pets, low SATs,
ripped right through the return address.
The lightning forks indecisively,
the road not taken is the one we took
ending up in the same darn place anyway,
the mall of course, in quest of coasters,
sugar substitutes, prefab rags, crystals.
When I was a child, my playmates were all lunatics.
They'd scamper across the lawn in their electric
chair lunatic hair ready to share a big
rubber band. No one but a dog had been shot
into outer space but we were blasted
in our orbital pj's. Some people should not
be exposed to modern art or permitted
gum. Set on fire, a lunatic often
continues to hum which is frowned upon.
After a while I noticed some afforded
special status and took no part in snow
removal. If you spoke to them, you'd doubt
your own existence so shoveling through
a glacier seemed preferable. Once you get

to the middle, it's not like living in a diamond though.
It's like being swallowed by a broken lightbulb
and all you hear is that soothing, on-hold
lost spaceman music. You know, the kind they play
to get you to buy useless products, rocks
that grow hair, deodorizing saints to hang
from the rearview, indulgences, all because
of that floating frozen numbness, immunity
to credit card debt, the cosmetic girls
with blue lips offering an atomized squirt.

Rose Prick

The others in the rose garden
are arguing about Blake, whatever slept
in their heads struggling to wake. The roses
are anything but blasé yet they stay asleep,
so few of them in November any seems
an unlikely plenitude. No one
will ever want to kiss me now, thinks
the girl in the burn unit and No, no,
shout the sleeping roses, some with thorns
eyelash soft, others beetle-cankered.
Why aren't we more terrified of sleep,
of consciousness extinguished and no
guarantee of return? Because of
consciousness extinguished and no
guarantee of return? The roses
never wake either, they lie in plastic sleeves
atop the coffin asleep, take part
in brazen backseat sex asleep,
whatever secret's whispered into their labia,
they'll never repeat. And when they wither
like fire made of water, you will wither too,
pestered by contradiction. A world so full
of detail yet so vague, a spot
of blood so red rubbed away.

Oddly Folded Bird

Suddenly my hunger names itself
beef and barley soup. Previously
it had been nnugharrh and grrr and a slit schwa
so obviously I was on the mend. Funny
how stuff comes to rescue me. Squirrel
who dashed out of the wheel-well—
I hadn't laughed in days. Ice lenses
on puddles to break to restore my faith
in the happiness of shattering. I thought
it was all a contest who could feel worse.
About carrying fists in your pockets
and adding to the don't list. Warts.
But hello libidinous cabbage,
I see your core. Hi there piece of rope
dropped from a truck, I see your inter-
rupted destiny. To lose the ability
to welcome is never to take terror
into your heart, never see its yellow eyes
in the dark left ventricle. What the hell is that?
asks the tech rubbing the electric wand
over the cold jelly on my chest. My glee,
I tell her, my secret tulip bulbs.
I want you all to stand up
and sing something when I die.
I believed in unplugged purposes.
I believed mercy was a substance in the water
like what turns flamingos pink.
Please tell my wife I wasn't always mean,
blaming her for the broken answering machine,
bitching about lint. Help her remember
how clean I was for a junkyard,
how I bought her that French saddle,
how much I loved her for a chunk of coal.

Grave Tour

I was hoping for some contact with the natives,
the ones who built these sepulchral impediments,
an iron pianist whose music issues
from a hole in the head,
a big marble ball.
This is how they honor their dead
even when the ground's too frozen to make a dent,
the fauna dependent on handouts,
a stake become a snowman's spine,
a hardy folk kaput nonetheless
after a long winter's whooping, an even longer spring
when the world declares its need for psychotherapy.
Mortality is the subject of which I sing
and know nothing about, it's always someone else's
who won't return my calls, who never writes
except homilies in frost.
The silver tray drops in the foyer,
Mother must be revived with rosewater,
the flowers are left to go scummy in the vase,
none go back until they can forget
or go back not to
or some fuzzy combination of the above.
The house grows quiet as an upside-down mug,
the ghost ship circumnavigates the globe,
the comet disappears for 57 years.
But new, raunchier advocates are on the way
to take the place of those vanished
in the mist or seemingly imploded to bits
so one night a single ghostly thumb may print itself
upon your brow not unlike a lily,
you too readied for departure
into the abyss that is always changing
and yet a steady nothingness
behind the cheesesteaks of Philadelphia,

the needle of Seattle,
New York City's addled rush,
inevitable, lush, sometimes grave as a kiss
between friends who would like to be so much more.

Exit Exam

Difficult to believe what hurts so much
when the cement truck bounces you
off a tree trunk
is not solid knocking solid
but electron cloud repulsing electron cloud
around the overall emptiness of matter,
a clash of miniscule probabilities
in the beehive of the void.
Somehow you're only scratched and bruised
but the driver's in agony,
no license no immigration paper
a picture of his wife still in Oaxaca
five kids he sends money to
so you try to assure him you're okay
look not hurt
hopping foot to foot
which only seems to him
you've got trauma to the head
or were already loco
either way problemo.
Your bicycle bent,
he lifts it tears in his eyes
which are mirrors showing everything
on fire in black water.
This is the universal language of bent bikes,
something large and tragic writ in small words
while the world burns in black water.
Nothing will repair it
is not true
but now is not the time to bring that up.
You are both golden
pepperoncinis in the vinegar of life.
So piquant, so sad.
There is a wound where you bonked against the tree
and the tree, as usual, deals with its injuries

in good humor.
A bird in its branches had just come to life,
hideously bald, eyes unopened bulging sacks,
too delicate, too helpless
yet there is a concept of the cosmos forming
in its tiny skull. It gapes and mother
regurgitates nutritious worm.
It grows a black miter and blue belly.
Nest formation, a couple false starts then presto!
It calls its mate radiant toy.
Its mate calls back radiant toy.
It gets trapped in the science building for an hour.
Still, it understands no more
than we do that voice coming toward us
in our dented sorrow, our dark dread
saying everything will be okay.
Bright opening bright opening
where does it come from?
How can we get there?
And if we do
will we be petrified or dashed to even smaller pieces,
will we be released from the wheelhouse
or come back as hyena or mouse,
as a cloud or rock
or will it be sleep's pure peace of nothingness?

******

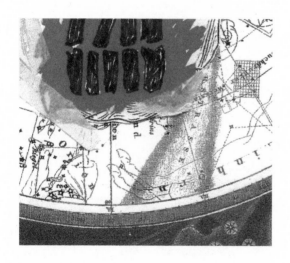

Afterward
(Little Evening Sermon)

By the seventh time the story was told,
the girl stood naked in the sprinklers
and the fighter pilot had flown on E
through Russia. The bear could almost talk,
the crippled dog could almost run and we
could almost love each other forever.
Funny word, forever. You can put it at the end
of almost any sentence and feel better about
yourself, about how you've worked in a spray
of sparks accomplishing almost nothing
and feel that's exactly what the gods
intended, look at the galaxies, spilled
milk, their lust and retrograde whims.
What was it you were promised? I'm sorry
if it turned out to be a lie. But the girl
really did drink fire from a flower,
the dog did leap a chasm, days advanced
and the stars spun through our umbras
and threw their backward light upon
the bent, deniable, rusted, unaffirmable,
blank-prone forever.

ACKNOWLEDGMENTS

Some of these poems appeared in these magazines:
*American Poetry Review, Bat City Review, Conduit,
Crazyhorse, Denver Quarterly, Gettysburg Review, New Ohio
Review, Octopus, Paris Review, Ploughshares, Poetry, Tin
House, Threepenny Review, Zoland*, and *Zyzzyva*. I thank
those editors.

"Gawker" owes much to Ben Gocker.

Thank you, Neal Nixon,

Mark Levine, Emily Wilson, Cole Swenson, Dora Malech,
Jim Galvin,

Tony Hoagland,

Mary Carr,

and Mary Ruefle.